CASH ENVELOPES: YOU'VE NEVER HAD SO MUCH MONEY

BONNIE LACY

FROSTING ON THE CAKE PRODUCTIONS

Any questions about the book, or to contact Bonnie, please email:
bonnie@bonnielacy.com

ISBN-13: 978-1-943647-14-9(Print)
ISBN-13: 978-1-943647-09-5 (E-book)

CONTENTS

Introduction   vii

1. Letter to Money   1
2. Being Honest   3
3. First Steps   8
4. Setting It Up   15
5. Running Smoothly—Or Not!   19
6. It's Never The End!   22
7. Letter From Money To Me   28
8. Resources   30

   Stay Connected   31
   Also by Bonnie Lacy   35

"I love money. I love everything about it. I bought some pretty good stuff. Got me a $300 pair of socks. Got a fur sink. An electric dog polisher. A gasoline powered turtleneck sweater. And, of course, I bought some dumb stuff, too."
~ *Steve Martin*

INTRODUCTION

I went shopping the other day. For clothes. I had booked several speaking events and needed some things—other than jeans and T-shirts. The owner at the shop helped me figure out some great outfits. I love them! I finally found a store that when I buy, I wear! And yeah, I spent some bucks—especially when I added in a great leather backpack for $98. It's beautiful, but a great price—right? (Secret? I still buy at thrift shops—I love those too!)

Yeah.

Let me take you back a few years to when my husband and I were in terrible credit card debt. I had about $30,000 on mine, and my husband had about the same. I had been in network marketing and they pressure you to buy the products so you can display and sell. I have so many baskets ... but that's another story.

Back to the clothes shopping.

The only time I have credit card debt now is when I'm publishing books and buying ads to promote those books.

When I paid for those clothes, I wrote a check for it all. I didn't overdraw my account. I didn't pay with a credit card, either! I have paid cash in the past, but with the backpack, I went over my cash envelope total.

Just wrote a check.

I walked to my car and started it up. Looked at the bag (I really liked what I bought. Those tops were so … and the backpack) and sighed a happy. No guilt, like when I'd get loose with the credit cards in the past. (No, I don't blame my bad choices on an inner little brat or name her. It's ME. All me.)

See, when I paid for those clothes that day, the money came from the Clothes and Shoes Cash Envelope that I had deposited into our checking account.

I didn't use the grocery money.

I didn't max out a credit card.

Have you ever stood at a check-out with your insides quaking because you couldn't remember the balance on your credit card? Have you ever heard the sales person say, "Your card won't go through?"

Yeah.

Me too.

There is always a line. Others waiting behind you hear those words.

Shame. Shame. Me too.

But not this time.

When I got home, I laid out those cute outfits on the bed to show Dearly Beloved.

In the past, I would have crammed them in my closet or under the bed. Then, when I wore them and Dearly asked, "Is that new?" I'd say, "This old thing?"

Lie, lie, lie.

When I wear one tomorrow, I can tell him where I bought it, how much I spent, and that I have two more, in different colors. (Or whatever.) He'll want me to model some. (But that's a whole other subject! Different book, maybe! ;o))

See, I love being excited to wear my new pretties instead of hiding them in shame and fear.

I'm free.

Hiding and keeping secrets is exhausting.

And I don't think my God wants me to live like that.

Hence, this book.

I'm letting it all out, so hopefully you can be as free as I am.

Come on in.

Oh, disclaimer—I'm not a CPA, a lawyer, an accountant or a financial counselor. I'm a human who really messed up.

But!

I can breathe freely now, instead of choking and feeling like someone is twisting my stomach. (It's not a good ab exercise, believe me.)

Let's do this together. Yeah, it hurts to look honestly at the damage. It's scary to look at the truth. I know. But the truth set me free, and it can set you free, too.

Let's do this!

ONE
LETTER TO MONEY

If you have read my nonfiction book, *Rage Rising: My Walk Through the Dark Tunnel of Anger*, you will remember I refer to Joanna Penn and her podcast on thecreativepenn.com when she interviewed Orna Ross, ornaross.com. They were talking about how Orna had people in a workshop write a letter to money. "Tell it what you think of it!"

My antenna went up.

I should do that.

And I did.

(I also went on to write a letter to Anger. You can read that in *Rage Rising: My Walk through the Dark Tunnel of Anger*.)

DEAR MONEY,

How do you start something like this? Addressing a letter to you, Money, implies that you are real or even an individual —a person.

You're just paper or metal, aren't you?

But if you're just paper or metal, then why do I think about you so much? And why are you so hard to earn or get?

Why do I get the feeling that *you*, Money, control *me*?

I love to spend you. I love to use you. I love to have the things you can buy.

When I don't have enough of you, I am scared or sad.

When I am sad, I can go shopping and I am happy again —for a moment.

But the moment dies away, and I am sad, so I go shopping again and again. Like an addict.

So Money, you do not own me. I am divorcing you. You are back to just being paper and metal to be used in building a life.

That's all.

BONNIE

TWO
BEING HONEST

Let's go back a few years …

Here came another bill I hadn't anticipated.

And another.

Bills due once a year used to terrify me. Bills due twice a year, ditto. I completely forgot about them until the envelopes arrived in the mail. I never could remember when they would be due.

I didn't have a system.

That was the first strike against us.

The second?

We didn't have the money to pay those once-a-year bills, because I couldn't remember when they were due!

On top of that, we were many thousands of dollars in credit card debt.

Anybody out there know what I mean? Know how I felt?

Terrified.

Gut-wrenching fear.

We lived every day, waiting for the bomb to go off. One more bill—or somebody sick, and a trip to the doctor would send our checkbook balance over the edge.

Somehow, we made it through those times. Not by selling our first child. Nor by living on the streets. And we didn't move back home with our parents.

Some of that living on the street stuff happens. And worse. Heartbreaking.

This book is about our journey out of the mess we had made and the power of the Cash Envelope system, in every part of our lives.

After several years of hiding credit card debt from each other, my husband and I opened up and spilled our guts, or more properly, told the truth! We each had major debt we had been hiding from each other for years.

I don't know what he thought would happen if I knew. I'm not even sure what I thought would happen if *he* found out.

Divorce? No.

Murder? Maybe.

No.

Shame?

Yes.

Embarrassment?

Yeah.

Puking It Out

But a friend convicted me to spill, to tell my husband the truth, no matter what. I needed to come clean.

It was scary.

I was ashamed.

Not sure what his response would be, I never gave it a thought that *he* might have almost the same amount of debt as I did.

When we both put everything on the table—telling the

truth—it was such a relief. Covering it up for all that time had filtered into other areas of our relationship and could have destroyed our marriage. Thank God it didn't go that far.

Freedom is such a powerful word. As we progressed into more and more honesty, the freedom we felt and embraced was so refreshing. Very empowering—both personally—and in our marriage.

Facing Reality

We had brought everything out in the open, onto the table. But where to go from there?

Gut-wrenching reality hit hard. How in the world were we going to pay off these cards?

Not only that, the rest of our financial world didn't stop so we could pay them off. Bills kept arriving in the mail. The cycle of day-to-day expenses rolled on: mortgage payment, electric bill, water bill, car payments. Food and fuel needs.

It hits me as I write this, how needy we had become. "We can't do without that car. We can't cut out the lawn service. Cell phones are our lifeline. We have to have a smart phone."

This nation and the better part of the world is focused on the next consumer fix. The next techie toy. We watch, with credit card in hand, for the big announcement of *the* upgrade. No matter what it is: phone, TV (the bigger, the faster, the better), video game, car, house, vacation, second home, camper.

It's all a game to see who has the best, the most, the biggest.

Jealousy plays a huge part. I didn't intend for this book to become a statement of plagues, but I see it in my life. With this book I hope to spew out my own plagues/sins and hopefully, help you with yours.

Writing brings its own form of reality and healing.

Hence this book.

I am opening up this dark secret to you, in the hope of helping you gain freedom in your finances and life.

But as I open up, I can and will heal, too.

If Nothing Changes, Nothing Changes

At a certain point, in becoming honest with Dearly Beloved, the relief was immediate.

After fessing up, the hardest part was making the changes that we needed, in order to crawl out of the hole we had buried ourselves in.

How to pay all this off? Declare bankruptcy? Some do. We didn't.

This looked like the Rocky Mountains looming ahead and us without a four-wheel-drive. We had to hike to the top. How to pay these credit card bills, plus keep a roof over our heads?

I am a writer, plus a huge reader, so I dug in, reading books recommended to me. (You can find a list in the Author Notes, under Resources.) Some applied to us, some didn't. It felt like we were starting over in our financial lives, and in a way, we were. Felt like we were buried alive!

But we didn't die!

When something like this happens, we always tend to think the worst.

We could DIE! Oh, no!

I'm laughing now, because I can. But at times it felt like we *might* die. It is heart wrenching, first of all, admitting to the stupid! But also, it crucifies our pride, our selfishness.

I saw myself in a whole different light.

I wasn't the diva.

When faced with my dad's death and then Mom's illnesses, I SHOPPED. I told myself, "I need to unwind. Life is so stressful."

What needed to change?

WHO needed to change?

Power

After fighting through truth and facing reality, where was the power?

First, where was the power to heal, to overcome?

Where was the wisdom?

In crying out to God, I began to forgive myself, my husband and those stupid ads that made me buy. (Right?)

And He helped me see the plan. Did He show me every step? No. Not all at once, anyway. But He led me, step-by-step, to where I am today. And He will continue to lead me, as I seek Him. He has the best plan!

Power came through honesty with myself, first off.

Power came in opening up to Dearly Beloved. It strengthened as we consulted each other—instead of making decisions in secret. Step-by-step, as time passed, we gained power in those decisions and following God's plan.

THREE
FIRST STEPS

Our first steps needed to be baby steps as we learned this new way of living and banking and financing. We had plunged headlong into creating debt, without thinking. Our childishness had driven us to buy, buy, buy. Now we needed to rein ourselves in and teach ourselves to grow up—and that we couldn't get everything we wanted.

I needed to learn to recognize that when I spied a sale on shoes and I wanted to jump up and down, I had to tell myself *no* because actually I *needed* those *books* about how to get out of debt. (See how I am? I tried to get myself *into* more debt by buying books on how to get *out* of debt!) I even wanted to buy more than I needed at the grocery store. (It's food, right? So, I need to buy it!)

Opening bills in the mail, like car registrations due once a year, really got me off my behind to take those first steps.

Get Out The Calculator

I'm not really sure where the idea came from to start using cash envelopes. Probably something I flitted over in my desperate reading. (See resources.)

My parents had never spoken of them that I remember, although my sister remembers more than I do.

When I got out the calculator, reality hit hard. Seeing numbers in black and white (or red and white) hit home.

That moment truly is overwhelming to anyone who has been there.

There are plenty of books about how to pay off credit cards. They recommend paying off the smaller ones first, then pushing those freed-up payments to add onto the payment for next smallest balance, and so on.

But this book is primarily about cash envelopes.

So ... get out the calculator. Get out the checkbook or credit card statements if you pay for anything with your credit card.

We have a joint account that I use because Dearly Beloved is often out on the road, using the business account. So, our cash envelopes are based on the joint account only. For home and personal use only.

Go back six months in that checkbook register or online. Create categories as you go: Groceries. Fuel for the car. Water bills. Lawn Maintenance. (That one seems like a luxury and it is, but it is my gift to me as Dearly Beloved is gone overnight five to six nights a week.)

Every grocery store amount gets recorded as "Food," including Walmart. Yes, we all know that it is easy to toss a book or shirt in the cart there. But just add Walmart entries in as "Food," to keep things simple.

Then total up every category. Every time you paid for fuel. Every check for shoes, clothing, movies. Every charge for eating out.

Also separate out doctor bills. Any medical bills. Pharmacy.

Do you want to save for Christmas?

How much do you spend for gifts other than Christmas? Birthday gifts? We have many grandkids now!

Remember! What you set up at first can be revised later— after you live with the system for a while. Yup, a later chapter addresses that.

I CAME up with these spending categories, which became my Cash Envelopes:

Fuel for car

Groceries

Christmas

Doctor

Gifts

Mary Kay (Yup—everything.)

Eating out

Shoes

Clothing

Water bill

Vitamins

Lawn service

Vacation

Entertainment

Car registrations

CPA

LOOK OVER MY LIST. Yours won't be the same, but there'll be similarities. You may not use Mary Kay! You might not buy Vitamins (or food supplements) on a regular basis like I do. We live in small-town-USA, so our Water bill comes from a cash envelope. "Vacation" is for any small trips we may take: to see the grandkids, a camping trip, or towards the Big Vacation. It is such a pleasure to want to go on a movie date to see the latest blockbuster, dig into the Entertainment envelope and presto: we have enough to have a burger too, from our Eating Out envelope!

We have a trucking business, so our cell phones, car and pick-up payments and maintenance, are paid by the business. This is a great reason to start your own business, just as long as the deductions are legitimate.

I also create temporary envelopes for upcoming expenses: piano maintenance, new glasses, the next freezer full of beef.

Also, you will hopefully see (further into this book) that when I deposit our paycheck, there are some bills that are easier to pay by check. I have a weekly system of when I pay those utility bills, internet, tithe. Utilities are set up on a budget plan, so that's easier paid by check, too. When we started this system, our home was paid for, so there was no mortgage payment. And we do have a Netflix account set up on a credit card. (Yeah. There are definitely some bills that need to go there.)

Okay. Now look over what you actually spent over the last six months in each category. Take the Grocery category, for example. We are empty nesters now, so ours won't be the same as some of you with several kids at home. There are many ways to save on food: gardens/canning, coupons, etc. Be brutal.

Did you spend $200 per week? $400?

How often did you get paid during those six months? Once a month? Twice? Every week?

Let's say you spend $100 per week on food and get paid weekly (gonna make it easy). You need to put $100 in your

Grocery cash envelope every week. If you get paid monthly, you'd need to put in $400. If your actual total is $289 for your envelope, you can round it up to $300 if you want.

Add up what you spent in each category, until you get through them all. Also add in your own categories. Do you purchase fabric on a regular basis? (If you do, I have some I'll give you!) Then make a category for that and figure out how much you'd need per paycheck.

This takes a bit of time but stick with me. My husband now brags on this system to his pool partners or anyone else who will listen! That. Is. Huge.

You will need to figure out which bills are easier to pay with your checking account, even when you pay for most things with cash. Some bills you might need a receipt for, so that would be your check. I note when each bill is due, and—this was huge—I make out a payment schedule. No more terrifying surprises!

Other "checking account" bills for us are utility or insur-ance—bills that are not local. Just easier to send a check rather than run an errand long-distance! (Although, I love road trips!)

If you get paid twice per month or once a month, adjust accordingly. If you get paid monthly, you will have more cash on hand on payday, which is sometimes harder or more tempting. But divide it out the same way, with however often you get paid. You might then want to divide out—say—your food envelope again, so you have just that amount available for a week at a time. If you are a good steward of cash, maybe do the major shopping once a month, and pick up bread, milk and fresh foods weekly, saving that amount each week for those items.

Gather The Envelopes

No, really.

Gather envelopes. I use the ones from my credit card mailings, since I pay those bills online. Or when you get credit card applications in the mail—there's always an envelope.

Yup. I'm cheap now.

Write the category on the outside: Groceries, Fuel, or Christmas, and how much goes in each, from every paycheck.

Find a folder or expandable file to keep the envelopes in. Keep it in a specific place because this is the guts of your household spending.

I have a portable file—plastic with grooves for file folders. It came in extremely handy when we lived in our camper for two months, while we waited to move into our new home.

Otherwise, keep your file in an office, closet, or wherever you sit to pay your bills. Keep your incoming bills in the file, too, if you'd like. You'll always know where they are!

Getting Organized

After you get your folder and envelopes set up, the next step is to create a monthly schedule of what bills you pay in each week. I made one on the computer for each week, since we get paid weekly. For instance, we always pay our electric bill in the third week of the month. It's due the last week, so we have a small cushion.

On my schedule there's a line for each week, from the first of the month to the end of the month, and what bills need to be paid from that paycheck *and when*. You could even slide your schedule template into a plastic cover and check off the paid bills with a marker, then wipe and reuse each month. I have a stack of scratch pads and sometimes I just use those. Again, I use what I have. I didn't go out and pay big money for a beautiful, packaged system.

FOUR

SETTING IT UP

Now comes the big day! How does all this fit together and actually work?

Read on!

Pay Day—How Much In Each?

Okay. The check is on your table—whether it is actually there, or it has been auto-deposited into your account.

You have already figured out how much goes into each cash envelope. Now figure out how many twenty dollar bills, tens, fives, and ones you will need. You have to break it down, because when you go to the bank to get your cash, they need to know.

Say you need $250 for Food, $30 for Christmas, $100 for Fuel, $10 for Eating Out. (I know these are not all of what you'd need, but just for demonstration's sake.)

You should get three one hundred dollar bills (two for Food, one for Fuel). How much do you still need for each envelope? Now figure out the twenties. You'll need three of them—two to put toward Food and one for Christmas. What's left? Tens—three (one to finish Food, one to fill out Christmas, and the one for Eating Out). A total of $390.

Yes, that takes a bit of time to figure out, but it helps to have it all done before you go to the bank. I write how many of each denomination I need on a Post-It note.

You could even break down the one hundred bills further into twenties, if you want. Whatever you are comfortable with.

Now. Time to go to the bank.

It's a little humbling at first, to walk in with your paycheck and denomination list. They don't ask ... they just sweetly fill your request. You get used to it and so do they.

You deposit the paycheck, minus the $390 cash back for your cash envelopes. What stays in your account at the bank is for those bills that are easier to pay with checks, like I noted in a previous chapter. I pay the credit card by online from that account. Also, my haircuts, our car insurance, utilities, and a few other specifically budgeted expenses.

Then go right home and distribute the cash into the envelopes, according to how much you wrote on the outside of each envelope: $250 in the Food envelope, etc.

As the Clothing envelope fills, you might be needing a jacket for summer, or your underwear might be getting ragged. Now you can dip into that envelope. But, have a conscious plan, so you don't run out and play. This is hardcore. No using the credit card.

When Dearly Beloved comes home and tells you he had an especially great day, you can celebrate because your Eating Out envelope is well stocked!

Honesty Pays

Yes, honesty pays.

The biggest challenge is to be honest with yourself.

Doesn't matter what other people think, even though we care. We have to do what is best for our own finances.

I used to be nervous going to the bank when I first set this up. But now when I go to the bank to get the cash, it's no big deal. I sometimes bring cash from say, my Clothes envelope for deposit, to pay toward a new pair of jeans I just charged to the credit card. Pay it back right away.

The bank tellers don't ask.

There will be times when you might need to borrow from one envelope for some reason: the holidays took their toll, a bill was bigger than usual, you found a deal on something. That's okay. Just be careful. It can be very easy to fall back into the old financial addictions. Still, I never borrow from the Medical envelope, the Food, the Car Registration, or a couple of others.

The section above, Being Honest, pays here and now. If I had hidden my debt, this never would have worked. I would still have had secrets and deep dangerous wounds. And if we hide these things, they never heal.

Grocery Trip

Well, here we are at our favorite grocery store and hopefully with a list in hand. Never go without a list!

Let's say there is $250 in our Food envelope. That is what we have to spend this week. (Again, this is just our example.)

The first trip or so can feel very humbling. I scribble on the grocery ad or in my journal the cost of every item in my cart as I drop it in, adding it up. I round each item up to the nearest dollar amount to allow for tax. Even though we don't have tax on food in Nebraska, there will be some items— toilet paper, paper towels—that are taxed. This way I'm not surprised at the checkout. You have a slush in anticipation of any tax. And I might have added wrong!

Stick to your list.

There are a few weeks, due to a Christmas ham or holiday leftovers, when my list isn't as long as usual. I use those weeks to buy the large package of sliced American cheese, if we're close to running out. Or an extra box of the trash bags we like—everyone else must like those too, because they are almost always out of stock where we shop. If they are in stock, I buy extra and adjust something else. If I'm not really out of flour, then I don't have to buy it. I purchase it on sale and store it in the freezer. (Freezing it kills any bugs that might be lurking in all that powdery goodness!)

I almost always buy extra baking products—sugar, flour, powdered and brown sugars—when they are on sale during the holidays. I have a pantry. If you don't have a pantry, that's okay. I have used under-the-bed storage or a linen closet for that. Yeah. Be creative!

Usually I only purchase bacon when it's on sale. I buy several pounds and freeze it.

Watch your ads and take advantage of prices. I don't know every price, but I do shop the ads.

We have a small grocery store close by that has great ads, and that is what I use to shop from. If I happen to be in a larger town farther away, I check their price leaders and shop their ads.

It's humbling, but a very good feeling when I check out. I know how much it will cost, and it's in my envelope. There are no surprises, unless you have little kids and they toss something in the cart without you catching them!

FIVE

RUNNING SMOOTHLY—OR NOT!

As with anything, something breaks down or falls apart. This is just a system that sometimes needs to morph over time as your life changes.

If It Doesn't Work—Fix It!

As I said before, there will be adjustments. This system evolves as your finances evolve. Here's an example. I used to have an envelope for Real Estate Taxes when we owned our previous home, but we purchased a new one, and now the taxes are included in the mortgage payment.

Still, I kept the total cash amount that I get at the bank the same. I just pushed that amount to the Medical envelope—or another crucial one.

Adding Other Envelopes

There might also be times when you need to add another envelope, as life changes.

I added one recently when I realized that our oldest

grandson would graduate from high school in three years. I want to be able to give him some cash for whatever he plans to do then.

I decided on the amount I want to give him and did some figuring. There are 156 weeks until he graduates, so I divided the amount by 156. That gave me the amount I need to add to the new Graduation Gift envelope each week.

Actually, I rounded it up a couple dollars—as we have ten grandkids. There will be 2-3 years between some of them, but two of them will graduate a year apart, so I wanted to allow for that.

Also, as the envelope fills, I have plans to set up a bank account. I'll funnel the cash there through our checking account as the envelope fills—again and again.

Some people might think doing it that way—depositing cash into a checking account to get the money into a mutual fund account or wherever—is a little too complicated or too many steps. I agree, it seems that way at first. But I have made a commitment to this system and it doesn't seem that hard anymore.

Doing things this way also slows down my spur-of-the-moment, jump-without-looking decisions and it can be reversed very easily when I come to my senses—there's no running back to a store to try and return something!

Most of us have become so insistent on convenience and microwave habits (I gotta have it fast and now!) that something that might take an extra step seems intolerable! But as I see these envelopes fill up and I check off my spending goals, it is all worth the extra work.

Stealing

Stealing.

From other people?

Uh, no!

Stealing from other *envelopes*!

And, yes I do that.

Stealing from the Lawn Care envelope when it's January and there is snow on the ground, is totally fine. I use it as a small savings account, which comes in handy.

Stealing a little from Entertainment is okay. But not so much that you lose date night.

But never, never, never steal from Medical or Water Bill envelopes.

Or Grocery. Or Fuel.

Then you could find yourself up against a bill without cash in an envelope!

SIX
IT'S NEVER THE END!

I don't know if you are like this, but I enjoy reading how the idea of a book came about, or what the author went through to write it.

In this case, I know many of you already know what's involved in setting up cash envelopes or something similar.

But everyone is different. Every system is different.

Thank you for checking out mine.

And thank you to my reader team. This book is short, but other books haven't been so short and reading them takes a lot of time.

Thank you to my editor, Kathy Tyers Gillin. You are always willing. Please keep on teaching me—there is lots to learn!

Thank you to my parents, who lived a frugal life as farmers—never knowing how the crop would turn out when the seed was dropped into the ground. But never losing faith in the One Who is Ever Faithful.

As always, thank you to my family—my Dearly Beloved, my kids, my grandkids.

Thanks be to God!

Ongoing Change

It's not hard to set cash envelopes up, but sometimes just reading the steps is all we need to get started. It's not so daunting.

Some tips in this book may seem juvenile to some readers, but remember that we all started somewhere. I had cooked minimally growing up, mostly beanie and weenies, so when I got married, I gleaned a lot from my mom and mother-in-law—both good cooks. I started where I was at.

And you can, too.

Realizing Benefits

There are so many obvious benefits to operating finances with the Cash Envelopes system.

1) MORE CASH Than You'll Imagine

I know the subtitle for this section sounds hyped-up, but it's true.

Once this system was in place and had been running for several months or more, I almost felt someone was planting cash in my envelopes.

Crazy … but it adds up fast.

As long as I don't steal from them.

2) CONFIDENCE/NO Fear

There is still a mild panic when I get a bill like a car registration.

Then I go to my envelope and there is the money, just waiting for the arrival of that bill!

Often, there is more than enough, which is my financial mantra, "I have more than enough." Or, "He is my Shepherd, I shall not lack."

There is peace.

There is confidence in a system that has worked for several years now.

There is no lasting fear when I pull a bill out of the mailbox.

3) POWER

There is power in this system.

A budget never worked for us. Well, maybe for a while, but for some reason, using cash envelopes keeps our spending in line and it's easy to stick to. It's not some obscure amount listed on a budget. It's hard cash. When it's gone, it's gone.

It might not be for everyone, but it works for us!

Trust God, Not Envelopes

Every time I sit at my desk to fill the envelopes, I thank God for the cash and the income to be able to do what I do: fill each envelope every week, anticipate savings, look forward to gifting grandkids, not overspending at Christmas.

I pray over the money, asking the Lord to bless and sanctify the cash to the use of our finances.

And He does.

Starting Over? Well, Not Quite

Recently we signed the mortgage for a new house. A *lot* of money.

During the whole process, fear rose up—every time the

lending institution asked for another document or proof of ownership or insurance.

I remember years ago when we first moved to Omaha—maybe forty years ago—I didn't have a credit card. Everywhere I shopped, whether at Target, grocery stores, or fabric stores, they required a credit card to be able to write a check. I hated that. When it was my turn at the cashier to write the check, they'd request the credit card for ID purposes, and I didn't have one. We'd have to go into this long debate, holding up people in line behind me. "Do you want me to shop here or not?" (I felt like I had some sort of power or worth that those big stores would actually want my business! That I was so important to their bottom line!)

Money rules this Earthly kingdom.

Dearly Beloved and I were just talking about that today, how money is a big engine in medicine—driving, say, cancer treatment. Every industry seems driven by money. People are victims, and money is the thief.

And sometimes money doesn't really have any worth, any meaning. It's just paper. It's just metal.

It wasn't until I started to use the Cash Envelope system that I realized we can have emotions tied to that cash, those coins.

When I used to be $30,000 in debt, the only time using a credit card made me emotional was when it was maxed out, and I worried when I handed my card to the cashier. Worried that it would be rejected in front of all those people in line behind me, to say nothing of the cashier.

Before that it was just a honeymoon of spending. When I bought groceries, if I knew I would pay with a credit card, I'd toss in a new shirt or a travel coffee cup. No problem. It was on the credit card.

When I started using cash from my grocery envelope, at

first there was fear. Did I have enough? Did I overspend? This was when I started adding up everything as I tossed it in my cart, so there wouldn't be any surprises at the register.

The subtle but powerful thing I noticed was that when I handed over the cash, there was almost a spiritual attachment to it as I dropped it into the cashier's hand. A grief. Anxiety. A love? Would I ever get more? Was this all I'd ever have? Was there ever enough?

I wanted more.

Check yourself. Is there a difference in emotion when you pay by cash rather than by credit card?

I grew up very content. We always seemed to have enough.

But. My mom worked outside the home at a time when it wasn't popular for women to do that. She was a nurse, so I imagine she earned good money, but that was the trade-off. We never took vacations except to visit her family. Dad farmed, which wasn't always profitable. It provided a wonderful place to live—in the country. I never felt deprived, although when I wanted to take ballet lessons, Mom explained that we couldn't afford it. That was okay. I had piano lessons and a little horse—a little Welsh breed that bucked me off on occasion. I had a tree-house in a huge cottonwood tree. I had all the drawing paper I would ever need.

But now that I've been on the Cash Envelope system, money does not rule my life. I rule the money. I plan where it goes. I spend out of the proper envelope and hardly ever rob from one envelope for another.

We just built a big beautiful home, and yes, we signed our lives away, or so they say.

But I have a knowing that we will be fine. I know my

writing will provide me with a good living. I just know. Is that blind faith? Maybe. I just know.

So, I think that right now, I am friends with Money. Never enemies.

Because of the envelopes, I can say to Dearly Beloved, "Let's go to a movie," and there is the cash to do that. Or we have the money to eat out—not every night or even every week, but there is freedom and joy in knowing I am not robbing from a pending bill to have that date night.

So, Money, I do not love you and I do not fear not having enough.

SEVEN

LETTER FROM MONEY TO ME

Dear Bonnie,

You have never had buckets and buckets of money. And you never seemed to have too much of a problem with me.

Yes, there were days when you didn't know how you'd pay for something important, like food. But you always had a positive and faith-based attitude toward me.

You are by nature a saver—not a hoarder. A giver, not stingy. But you are good at tucking some of me away.

Especially now with the cash envelopes.

There were times when you had money from your parents' farm and you seemed to spend right through it. (I did!)

If anything, you made yourself feel guilty when you did that—whether you bought some clothes for you, or something for the kids or grands— you had a hard time when you balanced the checkbook and beat yourself up when you saw where I went.

But you did nothing wrong. You never overdid it. Especially when you look at what others spend. Maybe they can afford it. You seem to know how far to go. When to slow it down and just sit on me.

You have a good eye for deals, and I will help you with that.

You need me to publish, and we will do that.

You are earning me in other ways, and that will help also. You haven't spent a cent of that. Maybe saving for a new computer or a writers' conference. But you will have the money you need to publish. Always be aware of not spending on too many things like software or other business tools. What you really need to do is write and create more products for the business to sell.

Books. Books might be your vice. But you always seem to read them. You enjoy them. You end up needing some for reference.

You will always have more than enough because that is where your faith is. The more you work and the more you believe and speak it out, the more you will have.

Thank you for allowing me to write to you this way.

ALWAYS THE BEST,
Money

EIGHT
RESOURCES

Looking back over time, I'm sure I have forgotten some resources that we used and gained insight from. If you have any, feel free to email me with your list.

1. *Big Magic: Creative Living Beyond Fear* by Elizabeth Gilbert. I listened to this one on audio and loved it so much, I bought the print copy, too.

2. *Rich Dad, Poor Dad* by Robert T. Kiyosaki.

3. *The Wealthy Barber* by David Chilton. I should read it again!

4. *The Total Money Makeover* by Dave Ramsey.

5. *The Financially Confident Woman* by Mary Hunt.

6. *The Richest Man in Babylon* by George S. Clason.

7. *Secrets of Six-Figure Women* by Barbara Stanny

8. *Real Artists Don't Starve* by Jeff Goins

I have a couple other titles but haven't read them yet. Maybe by the next edition of this book.

STAY CONNECTED

I greatly appreciate you taking time to read my work. If you enjoyed it: 1) Please leave a review wherever you buy books. 2) Or tell your friends about it! 3) Check the shelves of your local library. 4) Use hashtags #bonnielacy whenever you talk about my books online.

Do you like Christian Contemporary Fantasy? Christian, meaning following Jesus Christ. Contemporary meaning the characters drive cars, have phones. The Fantasy part? What's happening in the invisible world? What are the angels and demons up to?

If that's you, go to www.bonnielacy.com and sign up for my email newsletter by entering your email address. You'll receive the first four chapters from Book 1, Released in The Great Escapee Series and a reader's sheet for each book.

I'll keep you updated of new releases, giveaways, and any news I think might interest you. I promise to not blow up your inbox! 🤍

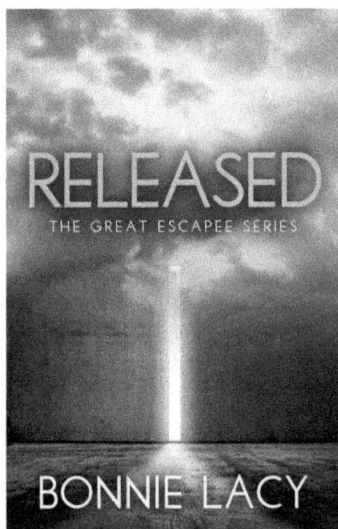

Your FREE book, Released!

Clarence is an ex-con. Nobody cares … except a tiny girl named Bea. He was locked up in prison for sixty years. Now he's free in a nursing home. Still imprisoned by his angry heart. He's been set up.

Bea's mommy, Katty, was abused by a former boyfriend. She follows her family's tradition for living and parenting. Until the boyfriend comes back for their daughter.

Released is a hero's journey through pain and guilt. Clarence goes where we all need to go—cussing and kicking at every step—to be released from shame.

Connect with me online: www.bonnielacy.com

Website: www.bonnielacy.com

Find my doodles and more on Instagram: @bonlacy

Twitter: @BonnieLLacy

ALSO BY BONNIE LACY

Nonfiction by Bonnie Lacy:

Rage Rising: My Walk Through the Dark Tunnel of Anger

E-book

Print

Cash Envelopes: You've Never Had So Much Money

Book - print and e-book

Workbook - print and e-book

Fiction:

Released

Rescued

Restored

Revealed

Redeemed

Resurrected

Box set: The Great Escapee Series

Released, Rescued, and Restored